It's a Jungle Out There

Poems and Drawings by Mukesh Nangia, M.D.

Index

"laughter is the best medicine"

SLAY OR SPRAY ?

Super Sam

Super Sam can slay a dragon,
Sam, the hulk, can lift a wagon.
He can stop a speeding train,
He can train a sluggish brain.

Sam can tame a raging bull,
He can fly a glider.
He can fool a sly fox,
But he hides from the spider.

Identical Twins

Tina is Inna's twin sister,
Tina happens to be a minute older.
Physically they look very similar,
But, Tina has no good bone in her.
When people start to compare,
Tina gives a nasty glare.

Inna is sharp whereas Tina is sloppy,
But Tina keeps boasting,
"I am the original, she is my photocopy."

Dentists

In year two-thousand-fifty,
The dentists are going to be nifty.
In their drive-thru booth,
They will yank your tooth.

They will do a *tooth-wash*,
Have a *cavity-check* lane.
If you want another *filling*,
You can drive thru again.

Spiders

Slinky, stinky spiders,
Had a big appetite.
Poor bugs would hide,
And stay in at night.

The spiders were smart,
They had foresight.
Their Ad on the net read:
"Visit our web site."

Rhymes, No Reason

Twinkle, twinkle, little star,
I wish I had a chocolate bar.

Humpty Dumpty was very tall,
Lo and behold! He scaled the wall.

Jack was simple; Jack wasn't quick,
Ouch! He got burnt by the candlestick.

Baa, baa, black sheep,
Have you any wool?
No, sir, no, sir,
We gave it to school.

Peter, Peter, pizza eater,
Soon his belly was up to a meter.

Mary had a little pet,
Who got very sick and went to the vet.

Scientific Mind

I forget where I put my stuff,
I am weak in geography.
I used to have a vacuum cleaner,
Now that is history.
Carrying garbage and groceries,
Hurts certain parts of my anatomy.

You must have figured, if you are smart,
Dodging work is really an art.

TROUBLED   WATERS ...

Double Trouble

I woke up one morning,
I knew I was in trouble.
Instead of seeing one,
I was seeing double.

I had two teachers,
I saw four preachers,
Tons of candies in the jars,
And, I had doubled my cars.

I think, I took double the pills,
And paid twice as many dollar bills.

"I didn't want to slow down this much...."

Mutation Station

Please check out my latest creation,
I call it Mutation Station.

The grumpy man comes out laughing,
The frail guy is no longer huffing and puffing,
The simple lad solves equations,
The bully gets standing ovations.

If you don't believe you can try,
You'll turn into a handsome guy.

Guess Who?

Two hands do the dishes,
The other two do some chores,
Another pair is busy cooking,
And the last ones mop the floors.

So, whom did you guess?
Oh yes,
It's Supermom!

What's In A Name?

Mr. Brown was actually white,
Mr. Strong couldn't really fight.
Mr. Goldsmith collected cans,
Mr. Walker owned two vans.
Mr. Doolittle did a lot,
Mr. Swift was eventually caught.
Mr. Shipman dreaded the coast,
Mr. Baker burnt the toast.

Mr. Rose by any other name could be a stinky rose.
There is nothing in a name, I suppose.

Belly Watcher

I was overjoyed,
After I checked my weight.
I used to weigh 150 lbs.,
I had lost eight.

A few weeks later,
My son was playing doctor.
He listened to my chest,
And my belly thereafter.

I quizzed my son,
"Do you hear rumbling sounds?"
He said, "No dad, it keeps whispering,
I lost eight pounds!"

Tanned Man

After a lot of sun,

Totally tanned he looked.
He used to be a cook,

Now *he* looks cooked.

"LOG ON ...."

Computer Lingo

What is a computer?
A box with some *chips*.
Download a *virus*,
It *freezes* and flips.

You click on the *mouse*,
To get your e-mail.
Use the *browser* and the *cursor*,
To read a tale.

It has a *hard drive*,
It takes *software*.
You *surf* the *net*,
While stuck to your chair.

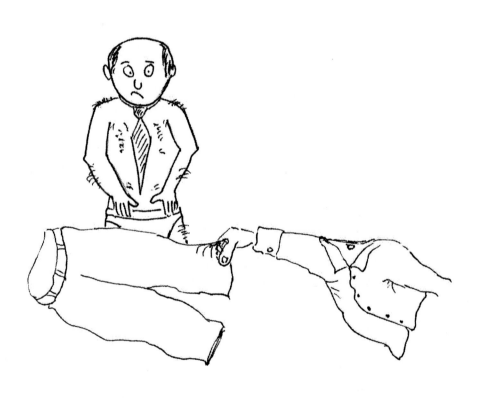

The Inside Story

The shirt kept pulling
the trousers' legs,
But the necktie
hung in there.
After the tug-of-war
was over,
The poor guy stood
in his underwear.

Sale Talk

Limited-edition mugs on sale,
Only a dollar for a pail.

It's a collectible from a different era,
Buy one and get one extra.

A special bonus gift inside,
A clearance sale! There is nothing to hide.

Everything must go! We lost our lease.
Don't just browse; come in please.

Fussy Eater

We have to eat broccoli,
That sounds so silly.
Having greens and beans,
Is not in my genes.
Peas are bland,
So *they* are banned.
Don't be mistaken,
I won't fall for eggs and bacon.
Name *one* dude,
That likes dairy food.

Only pizza is yummy,
Confirms my tummy.

X-Ray Vision

A broken bone,
A heart of stone,
A swallowed dime,
A perfect crime,
A thick hide,
And swallowed pride.
An ingested nail,
A bird from jail...

I catch them all,
With sheer precision,
Because I have x-ray vision.

"Can't fly now..."

Halloween

It is Halloween tonight,

Full of frenzy, full of fright.

People will scare the wits out of me,

It is going to make me pee.

Busy Bees

Cindy had to row her boat,
Mindy had to milk her goat.
Shirley left for work early,
Barbara cared for the sick elderly.
Sherry had some books to carry,
Terri had to tow a ferry.
Kylee liked to pick a fight,
Lizzie loved to show her might.

Near the mirror sat Nancy,
Wore some makeup, looked fancy.

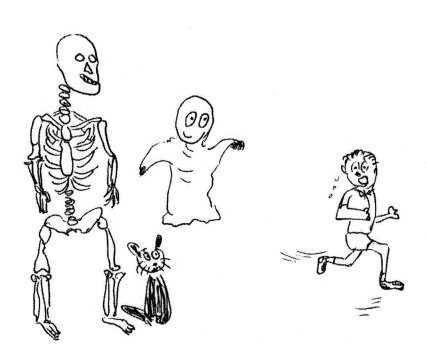

A Nightmare

On a dreary day,
We planned to go away.
Due to a navigation error,
We reached the tower of terror.

The tower was dark and old,
My feet were turning cold.
The bats began to fly,
It almost made me cry.

From nowhere came an owl,
The hyenas gave a howl.
The sweat was starting to pour,
I scrambled and opened the door.
There stood a scary skeleton,
I turned and started to run.

A chill ran down my spine,
When I read this sign:
'Enter if you dare',
Oh! What a nightmare!!

Then I heard a knock,
It was seven o'clock.
I was in my room,
After a night of doom.

Lazy Lou Logsdon

Lazy Lou Logsdon,
Loved to slouch.
Mere mention of work,
Would make him grouch.

He claimed
He mowed his lawn today.
But, guess what?
No one would vouch.

Magic Pill

He took the pill,
Not per protocol.
Soon he had grown,
About nine feet tall.

The scientist gave,
A strong antidote.
Now he can fit,
In the pocket of my coat.

Zoo Time

The kids were excited,
The teachers were delighted,
And so was the carefree crew,
It was time to visit the zoo!

David was making a howling sound,
Mike and Mark were monkeying around,
The chimps were hopping too,
Yes, we were in the zoo.

Tracy was pulling Kelly's hair,
Big Bob gave a cold stare,
The tiger ran to the loo,
It was fun to be in the zoo.

The animals were frazzled,
By all this commotion.
Their board of directors,
Passed this motion:
"We are innocent; we did no crime.
These kids should be made,
To do some *zoo time*."

Flying Cars

A hundred years
down the line,
The cars will
be flying.
The parents will literally
drop their kids off,
And the kids
won't be crying.

Pet Dinosaur

My pet dinosaur,
Is big, strong, and tall.
He scares the bullies,
And is always on call.

But there is one problem,
Buying groceries is no fun.
My favorite giant,
Eats by the ton!

Pop Culture

I drink pop,

I eat pop,

I suck on a pop,

I hear a pop,

I tune in to pop,

I live off my pop.

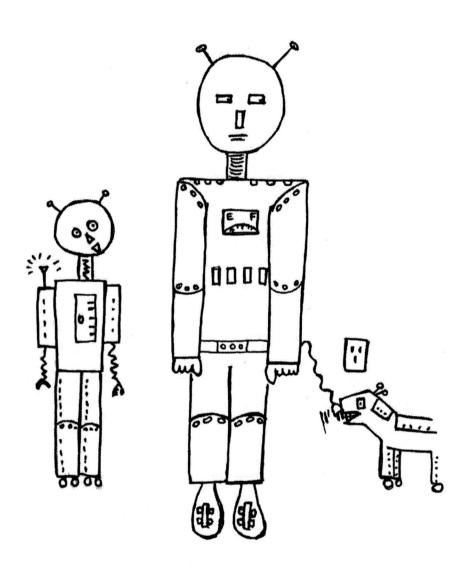

Robot

After much thought,
I invented a robot.

I taught it how to trot,
I showed it how to squat,
And how to clean a pot,
And care for my tot.

But believe it or not,
When I gave it a shot,
It wouldn't budge from its spot.
It wasn't plugged in—
I completely forgot.

Taco the Watchdog

Taco barks at Leo the leopard,
He isn't scared of the German shepherd.
He is on high alert night and day,
Taco chases the burglars away,

But when I vacuum my hardwood floor,
Taco hides behind the door.

Guessing Game

"I tap with a hammer."
You must be a physician.

"I pull out rabbits."
You must be a magician.

"I pull some strings."
You must be a musician.

"I watch their weights."
You must be a dietitian.

"I bless their souls."
You must be a mortician.

"I look them in their eyes."
You must be an optician.

"I color those cheeks."
You must be a beautician.

"I count my blessings."
You must be a statistician.

"I make promises."
You must be a politician.

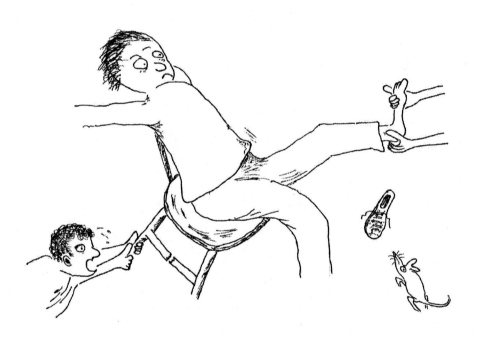

Mr. Chairman

John's sister Lottie,
Was really naughty.
She used her trick bank,
To come up with new pranks.

Once upon a time,
John got stuck.
He tried really hard,
But couldn't get up.
John had no clue,
He sat on crazy glue.

Sammy pulled John,
And Tammy pulled his chair.
Nothing seemed to work,
So they informed the Mayor.

They tried a few maneuvers,
Later, called the handyman.
Now John is famous,
As Mr. Chairman.

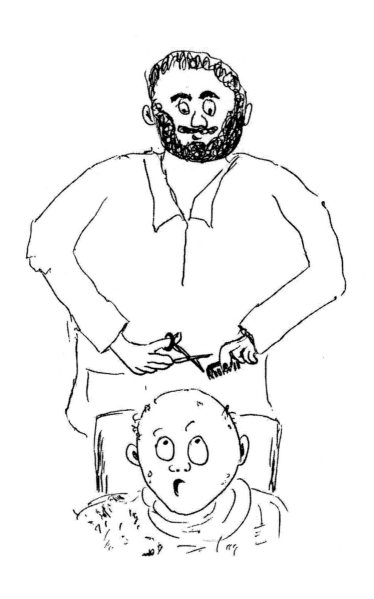

Hair Scare

I was put in a chair,
And draped with a smock.
I had no say,
I couldn't really talk.

He sprayed my head,
He reached for his clippers.
I closed my eyes,
After seeing shiny scissors.

I called for my mom,
I said a long prayer.
My hair was flying,
My head was bare.

Tony Tucker

My name is Tony Tucker,
I am a retired trucker.
These days when I am asleep,
I change lanes; I go beep-beep.

The other night I swerved,
When my truck hit a boulder.
I woke up on the floor,
With a very sore shoulder.

Vacation

The winter is over,
It stopped snowing.
The skies are bright,
The grass is growing.

The kids are hyper,
They are ready for the summer.
They ride their bikes,
They play street soccer.

The beaches are packed,
The pools look cool.
There is no homework,
There is no school!

Alas! Time flies,
When you want it to crawl.
The summer is over,
Who wants the fall?

The Lucky One

My fish is fortunate,
It can stay up very late.

It swims all day; it can go berserk.
No bills, no stress, no housework.

But, living in a tank can't be real fun,
I guess I am the lucky one.

Flying Saucers

When things get hot,
In our house.
I stay away,
From my grumpy spouse.

From their windows,
Peek our neighbors.
They see UFOs,
And flying saucers.

Time and Tide

You could waste your time,
You could spend every dime,
Have all the fun,
And give us parents a run.

But take this advice,
From a father to a son.
Time and tide,
Wait for none.

Kenneth Kent

Kenneth Kent,
Was very unkempt.

After bars of soap and jars of detergent,
He looked like a pleasant gent.

He got out of the tub,
He landed with a thud.
His clothes got filthy,
He got covered in mud.

This time they didn't go very close,
They power washed Ken with a long hose.

Lucy Bell

Lucy Bell had a wishing well,
Don't be greedy; it used to tell.

Lucy Bell didn't pay much heed,
She was overcome with greed.
She pulled out diamonds, gold, and crowns.
Tiaras, pearls, and shimmering gowns.

While reaching for the treasures, down she fell,
Such was the fate of Lucy Bell.

Plane Ride

In my throat, a lump I felt,
I quickly fastened my seat belt.

Very soon we were airborne,
In the clouds, on a chilly morn.

They served coffee with a few peanuts,
But something inside was wrenching my guts.

My glasses flew; my pupils blew,
My heart rate, through the roof it grew.

Due to major turbulence it felt like a slide,
Dear folks it wasn't a *plain* ride.

Testing Times

My cat had a CAT scan,
They did a PET scan on my pet.
My Labrador got a lab test,
I don't know what I will get?

A Pincushion

DPT, MMR,
Hep. B, H. flu,
Shot after shot;
I didn't have a clue.

The grim faced doc was
a man with a mission,
My little arm was
a big pincushion.

Whipped Cream

I took out my whip,
I let out a scream,
I whacked it a few times,
To get some whipped cream.

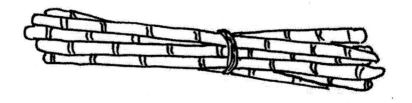

Unity

Let us work together,
End this senseless brawl.
"United we stand,
Divided we fall."

Let us build our nation,
Let us stand tall.
"United we stand,
Divided we fall."

Golf Ball

Fred and Ted were crying hoarse,
They wanted to be on the golf course.

Ted was an avid golfer,
Fred was an amateur.
Where Fred's strike would land?
You couldn't really be sure.

Fred was lagging behind,
While Ted was far ahead.
When Ted was done playing,
He had a golf ball on his head.

Lie detector

The lawyers went through layers of facts,
But couldn't catch the thief for his acts.
The thief was a good actor,
That proved to be the key factor.

They thought it was best,
To do a lie-detector test.
But the minute the thief spoke,
Even the lie detector broke.

BEFORE   AFTER

Hairy Harry

Hairy Harry,
Looked so scary.
Couldn't find,
A woman to marry.

One agreed,
On one condition,
A clean-shaven face;
Some aftershave lotion.

Harried Harry,
Swallowed his pride.
And meekly,
Followed his bride.

Cake Stealer

My dad doesn't eat much,
He watches his plate.
His tummy keeps growing,
With each passing date.

I stayed up one night,
To solve the puzzle.
He had cake on his plate,
With some milkshake to guzzle.

NOSY ROSY

Advice

Don't poke your nose,
Don't tread on my toes,
Don't get a swollen head,
I said.

Do follow your heart,
Do lend your ear,
And get off my hair,
I declare.

I Scream

How come Jane's plain ice-cream,
Grew some toppings?
Little did she realize,
They were bird droppings.

Miss. Twister

She twists the facts,
She twists my arm.
Then floors our parents,
With her charm.

I wish I had no evil sister,
I prefer to call her Miss Twister.

God Bless

O' honorable mister,
Give me a crumb.
I will put my brain to work,
I am not dumb.

If you can't give bread,
Give me some work.
I'll put in my best,
I will never ever shirk.

If you can't give work,
May God bless you.
I won't lose focus,
I promise you.

Dentures

Now I have my fake teeth,
Temperature dips don't matter.
I just put my teeth in a bowl,
When they begin to chatter.

Sneeze Attack

A deep-freeze,
A cool breeze,
And processed cheese,
Makes me sneeze.

A flock of geese,
A bunch of bees,
The willowy trees,
Make me sneeze.

God knows, I have
a sensitive nose,
After a hundred sneezes,
it's red as a rose.

Meteorite

A lone meteorite,
Came crashing down.
Now all of us,
Climb out of our town.

The Royal Magician

The royal magician,
Turned the throne into a bed.
Instead of getting an applause,
He was going to lose his head.

But, before the king could even punish,
The magician quickly made him vanish.

The Perfect Groom

Willie Wilson
looked weird,
He sported a
very long beard.

He proved to be
an ideal groom,
His wife used him
as a broom.

The Devil's Workshop

The rug was colored red,
The shoes were resting in bed.
The toys were on the fan,
The phone was in a pan.
The books were in the sink,
The clothes were splashed with ink.
The dog was covered in mud,
The garage was about to flood.

Oh, what a mistake their parents made,
To leave in charge the devil's brigade.

Excuses, Excuses

I would like to jog,
But the weatherman predicts fog.
The treadmill doesn't suit me,
It always kills my sore knee.

Tomorrow, I will walk a mile,
For that, let me rest awhile.

E Stir

Elaine and Ellen were eager,
To unearth the eggs on Easter.

Edna was utterly delighted,
Eight other kids were invited.

Elusive Edith explored the entrance,
Exhausted Emma eyed the fence.

Ecstatic Evelyn emerged with eight,
Envious Elizabeth tried to emulate.

Eventually, Emily entered an enclosure,
That looked very inviting.
She found eighty-eight eggs,
Now, that is *egg sighting*!

Cell-Phone Disease

Mel's arm was frozen in one position,
He wanted his doc to identify the condition.

The doctor diagnosed it with great ease,
He called it cell-phone disease.

Bozo

Bozo the clown,
Came to town.
He wore his gown,
Upside down.

His hat was sloppy,
His jokes were stale,
He got a big frown,
And no check in the mail.

Go Figure

Judging one's intelligence by one's color,

Really stinks.

Remember it's the brain and not the skin,

That thinks.

Cry Baby

The baby started crying,
On a moonlit night.
The parents kept trying,
To make the baby quiet.

The neighbors swarmed out,
On hearing loud cries.
But they were very willing,
To offer free advice.

They tried 'gripe water',
They brought a new concoction.
Oh, what a pity,
It brought no satisfaction.

Grandma thought of honey,
The baby took a slurp.
And slept like a baby,
After a big burp.

Food Court

The burger stuffed itself,
With meat and tomato.
On an adjacent table,
Lay a spicy bean burrito.

Pasta and pizza were confident,
Of winning the big event.
Hot dogs and cheese pierogies,
Were sure to make a dent.

The veggies were huddled in a corner,
Looking lost and dejected.
Sushi arrived from the Far East,
Glad to be selected.

Jimmy, the judge, was a health freak,
He stacked his plate with carrots and leek.

Blubber Boy

Jack was lazy,
Jack was slack.
He *loved* his couch,
And devoured his snack.

But all junk and no play,
Made Jack a blubber boy.

Black Tongue

Wilma Witch had a black tongue,
Her words came true; they really stung.

The planes would crash,
The boats would sink,
The trains would derail,
In a wink.

Once she uttered, "I'm dead right."
And sure enough, she died at the site.

Tummy Ache

Timmy had a tummy ache,
Every morning, sharp at eight.

A thorough check,
Revealed no cause.
The problem continued,
Without a pause.

The doctor suggested to open the tummy and see,
Timmy was suddenly tummy-ache free.

Rush Hour

Why am I?
Brushing and washing,
And honking and racing,
And jostling and shoving,
And dashing and crashing?

Why I am rushing?
Pumping my blood pressure up.
I need to slow down,
I need to let up,
Before I really blow up.

Looking Back

When I was four,
I played with wacky toys.
When I turned eight,
I played with weird boys.
When in my teens,
Roaming aimlessly was my routine.

Now I am an adult,
I feel like a fool.
I wish I had learnt,
More in school.

Pocket Money

Every day I have to holler,
I have to beg and plead for a dollar.
Once in a while my father,
Out of pity, gives me a quarter.

Asking for an extra dime,
Now, is that a big crime?
As you know, I am flexible,
I am going to settle for a nickel.

Strained Ties

I hate my necktie!
I hate my necktie!!

I can get it right,
Only after a few tries.
When it gets windy,
It aimlessly flies.
When it dips into food,
My heart just cries.

I think it is time to say
Bye-bye to my ties.

Slim Chance

I just turned fifty-eight,
I'm losing hair; I am gaining weight.
It is getting hard to find a date,
But, as they say, it's never too late.

Old Age

Every joint in my body creaks,
My teeth are loose; I have hollow cheeks.
I use a walker; I wear a hearing aid,

For daily needs, I need an aide.
I often leave my keys in the car,
Now, could you tell where my glasses are?

Garbage Bin

Hi! I am a garbage bin.
I have no next of kin.
People are utterly rude to me,
They throw rotten food at me.
They stuff me up to my throat,
They make me choke, they make me bloat.

I am very upset; I am really bitter.
This is no way to treat a collector.

Up All Night

The other night I could not sleep.

After flossing and brushing,
And washing and flushing,
And tossing and turning,
And longing and yearning,
And thinking and lying,
And bowing and praying,
And counting one thousand sheep___
I just could not sleep.

I tried eating and munching,
And scratching and punching,
And moaning and groaning,
And watching and phoning,
And cleaning and drying,
And baking and frying...

Complaining and crying,
I fell into bed in a heap
And finally got some sleep.

Didn't I tell you? It's a jungle out there.

It's a Jungle Out There

The summer has started,
It's time for country fair.
The zebras, the tigers,
And the bears are there.

The animals are going crazy,
They're all over the place.
The monkey missed the branch,
And ended up in a brace.

The elephants wore pants,
The rhino wants a tie.
The hungry hippo had to
Be happy with a pie.

The heavyset gorilla,
Broke the cozy couch.
Oops! The little kangaroo,
Fell out of the pouch.

The clown tried hard,
To make the lion laugh.
The ant took days,
To scale the giraffe.

The turtle fell and broke his shell,
But somehow saved his face.
The cheetah sprained his ankle,
And couldn't finish the race.

The geese were running wild,
They didn't really care.

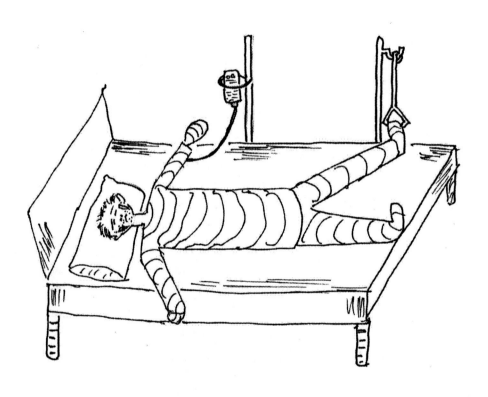

Accident Prone

Poor Fred rolled out of bed.
He cracked his ribs and bumped his head.
While shaving, he got a cut,
Then slipped in the tub and landed on his butt.

He got in his car,
But didn't go far.
At a busy intersection,
Had a head-on collision.
Due to serious trauma,
He is still in a coma.

Yeah Right

My dad said, "I can eat a whole cauli."
I asked, "really?"

My dad said, "I can milk a cow."
I exclaimed, "wow!"

My dad said, "I can ride a mule."
I uttered, "cool."

My dad said, "I can win a bullfight."

I screamed, "Yeah right!"

Alarm

The alarm of my alarm clock is alarmingly noisy,
It wakes up my neighbors and my whole family,
But for some strange reason,
It always spares me.

Umbrellas

Once upon a time,
The rain gods were sad.
It poured for days,
The forecast looked bad.

It wreaked havoc,
It caused mayhem.
There were umbrellas on people,
And people were on them.

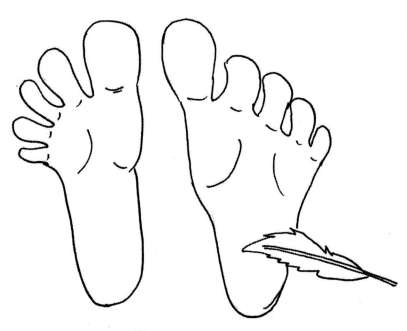

TICKLE TIME

Life Is Too Short

Touch a funny bone,
Make a bunny face.
Tickle someone's tummy,
Forgive and embrace.

Don't fight battles,
Try to win hearts,
Life is too short,
Why not get a head start?

House Grouse

The roof has some leakage,
The basement has some seepage.

The rug is worn out,
The bath needs a new spout.

The dishwasher makes a humungous noise,
The television has lost its voice.

The seeds need to be sowed,
The lawn needs to be mowed.

The garage needs a new door,
The kitchen needs a new floor.

Things aren't smooth I must confess,
Home, sweet home, is a total mess.

Little Mike

My friend Mike, riding on his bike,
Went to buy a cake.
On his way, he went astray,
And started playing with Jake.

They swung on the swing set,
And slid down the slides.
They played video games,
And had pony rides.

Soon it was dark,
Mike's parents got worried.
Little Mike panicked,
So poor Mike hurried.

He kept going straight,
He didn't lose track.
His parents were delighted,
To have him back.

Bald

I smeared magic lotion,
Drank a quart of herbal potion.
Tried standing on my head,
Tonic water; special bed.
Chanted mantra, practiced yoga,
Got some tea from Sumatra.

After trying them all,
I am totally appalled,
I am still quite bald.

Hurry Makes Curry

Mr. Murray,
Was always in a hurry.
Didn't realize,
That hurry makes curry.

He went out in a flurry,
Though his vision was blurry.
Alas! It was to be,
His date of expiry.

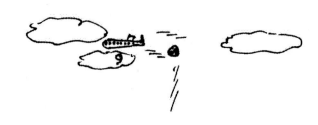

Soccer

The other night I had a dream,
I was leading my soccer team.
I kicked the ball so hard,
It landed overseas in my grandpa's yard.

The Perfect Recipe

Less whining,
More dining.
Fewer worries,
More curries.
Less coffee,
Some toffee.
Less panic,
Little manic.

Less video,
More sleep.
Just one or two,
Promises to keep.

I guess,
More or less,
You have the recipe,
For success.

My Baby

Each little step and every simple word,
Is a big achievement.
Your giggle and innocent laughter,
Makes some precious moments.

Sparkling eyes and a tender hug,
Makes hard work worthwhile.
I will go an extra mile,
To see your toothless smile.

Amateur Writer

I am an amateur writer,
But, I won't quit; I am a fighter.
Don't go by my looks,
I can write brainy books.

If rejected, you know what I will do?
I will just sit on you.

Storage

The Newton boys,
Had lots of toys.

They kept buying toys at a feverish pace,
And very soon they ran out of space.

They found an area of interest,
And turned that into their toy chest.

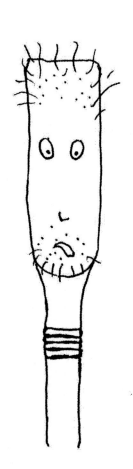

The Toothbrush

I am tired!

I am tired of cleaning you twice a day,
Going up, going down,
Cleaning the mess on my way.

I hate your stinky smell,
I am going through hell,
It is a thankless job,
Can't you see? Can't you tell?

I rub and I scrape,
I am bent out of shape.
I resent; I repent,
I want stat retirement.

The Troublemaker

My mom is a homemaker,
My dad is an undertaker,
My grandma has a pacemaker,
My grandpa is the peacemaker,
My sister is a born baker,
My brother looks like a skyscraper,

Guess who is the troublemaker?

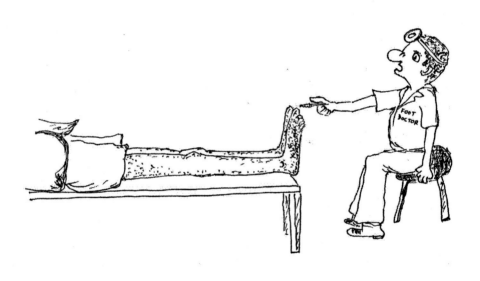

Body Care

Check your waste,
But watch your waist.

Brush your teeth before you sleep,
Think twice before you leap.

Wash your hands before you eat,
And scrub your stinky, smelly feet.

Heavenly Food

Snowflakes for breakfast,

Starfish for lunch.

Angel pasta for supper,

And some *sunflower* seeds to munch.

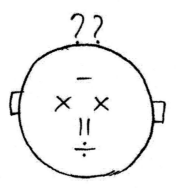

NON PLUSSED ...

Algebra

A plus B minus C times D,

Learn thy equation that's the key.

Hocus-pocus, abracadabra,

Now you know your algebra.

Dr. Gold

Dr. Gold was extremely old,

He could only treat coughs and colds.

He couldn't read his own scripts,

That is what my grandpa told.

The Iron Man

He pumped iron; he took an iron pill.
He donned an iron-armor; he had a strong will.

He was built like a bull,
He thought he was the toughest.
When he entered the science lab,
He couldn't fend the magnet.

Lighten Up

My eyes are shut tight,
Because the sun is too bright.
Leaving the bed doesn't seem right,
I like it dark as if it were night.
Spending hours after hours in bed,
Is such a delight!
I know my mom is going to say,
"Evil hateth the light."

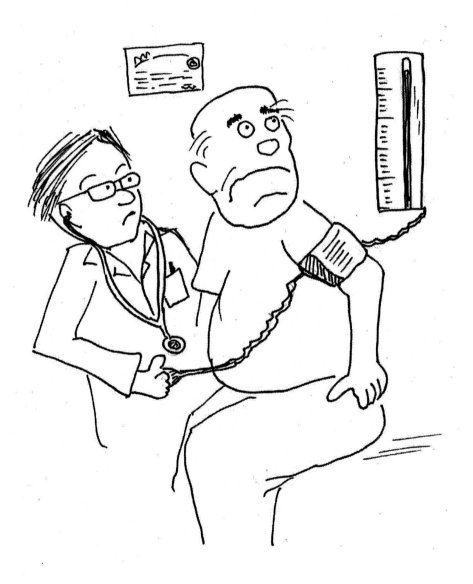

A Millionaire

When I was poor,
I worked very hard.
I earned every penny,
I had no credit card.

Now I am rich,
Things aren't much better.
Maids do all the work,
And I am getting fatter.

The Nap Kid

Anemia, leukemia, psychosis, neurosis,

I find them really confusing.

These books can surely wait awhile,

Presently, I shall be snoozing.

Beth mobile

On her bike rode Mary Beth,
After a few blocks she was out of breath.
She begged her mom; she struck a deal,
Now she rides her Beth mobile.

Kids

Elaine and Jane went to Maine,
They had yummy lobsters in the rain.

Ed and Ted wanted gourmet bread,
They had to settle for cookies instead.

Bart and Art went to the mart,
They had nothing but candies in the cart.

Allie and Abby were very close friends,
They were all about cool new trends.

Sherry and Mary loved their library,
They borrowed more than they could possibly carry.

Rhys and James invented a video game,
They hoped to enter the hall of fame.

I have to stop since it is getting late,
I will tell another yarn at a later date.